bless the dogs

photography by Vincent Remini

bless the dogs

The Monks of New Skete

CENTER
STREET

New York Nashville Boston

Hachette Book Group
237 Park Avenue
New York, NY 10017

www.CenterStreet.com

Printed in the United States of America
WOR

First edition: November 2013
10 9 8 7 6 5 4 3 2 1

Center Street is a division of Hachette Book Group, Inc. The Center Street name and logo are trademarks of Hachette Book Group, Inc.

The Hachette Speakers Bureau provides a wide range of authors for speaking events. To find out more, go to www. HachetteSpeakersBureau.com or call (866) 376-6591.

The publisher is not responsible for websites (or their content) that are not owned by the publisher.

ISBN: 9781455574261

Introduction

IN 1923 JEWISH PHILOSOPHER MARTIN BUBER penned a work that has become a perennial classic in the philosophy of religion: *I and Thou*. Taking issue with a narrow understanding of spirituality and mysticism, Buber presented God radically as the Eternal Thou, whom we can truly meet in all our relationships, and not only in solitude.

Readers familiar with Buber may recognize his inspirational force at work in BLESS THE DOGS. Buber's central intuition is that how we are in relationship with everything in our lives affects our experience of the sacred, and that we realize this effect in the very act of relationship, if only we are open. We humans can and do form mutually inspiring and beneficial relationships with our dog companions, and this experience colors every aspect of our life.

Yet the burden is not entirely on us to create or invent this marvelous reality. The tradition in which we stand holds that we already exist in a profound communion with all that is. Somehow, most of the time, we seem to stop growing in our awareness of this vital reality, of being truly at home in our bodies, and with each other, and in the cosmos. Constantly we become distracted, and rarely do we listen. Our dog friends, like life itself, are trying to get our attention. Maybe our canine connection is the missing link, a crucial invitation to respond to this great call to a richer, more abundant banquet of life that is already prepared and waiting.

If we had power over the ends of the earth,
it would not give us that fulfillment of existence
which a quiet devoted relationship
to nearby life can give us.

Martin Buber

bless the dogs

Part of the joy of getting a dog is naming it.
In Eden, Adam was given the responsibility of
naming the animals, and we have inherited his task.

A name not only defines — it expresses
the hopes we bring to the relationship.

Take care with a name; let its sound echo delight in
your soul, for a name will be the basis of countless acts
of communication that manifest your real feelings,
regardless of whatever else is said.

The vulnerability present in the smallest of God's creatures calls out to our noblest instincts,

triggering a desire to nurture and protect, to care for and understand. What we rarely imagine is how quickly the roles can change. Dogs have an astonishing capacity to respond to our own vulnerability, our sudden need for assistance. It's the flip side of a relationship written in paradox.

Often our feelings about dogs arise out of
deeply embedded memories from childhood
when dogs assumed a multiplicity of roles: playmate,
guardian, comic, even feared warrior down the street.
The depth of such sensibilities, both positive and negative,
points to the value of providing young children safe
experiences with dogs at their best, when connections
can be forged naturally, at their own pace.

Dogs have their own rhythms
that erupt spontaneously, even wondrously —

    a pair of amigos, for example, cavorting in the sand,
    relishing a rite of mock combat, transforming
    primal energies into a joyous dance of celebration.

Dogs mirror us back to ourselves in unmistakable ways if we are open, foster true understanding and change.

Dogs are guileless and filled with spontaneit unlike people, they don't deceive.

When we take seriously the words they speak to us abo selves, we stand face to face with the truth of the matte must learn to reflect on these words — they are inscrib bodies, in their expressions, in the way they approach a with us.

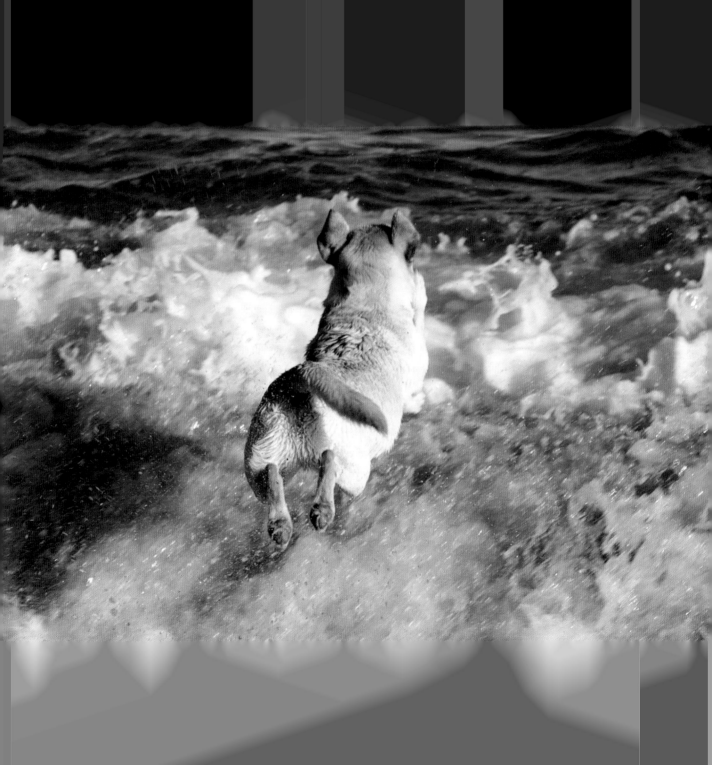

When you start and end your day with your dog by your side, life is lighter and brighter.

When life presents a challenge
that tempts us to discouragement, the clean love of a dog
has the power to draw us out of ourselves in a way that
brokers new confidence. Dogs don't lie, which is why we trust
their affirming presence to face the future.

There is a paradox in our understanding of the dog.

The more we learn of the dog's evolution — of its behaviors and instincts, of its needs and desires — the more we appreciate the mystery of its nature.

It is a mystery that will never be fully fathomed but that leaves us with an expanding sense of awe.

Though it is entirely natural for us to project human motives onto dogs, ultimately this is unfair: it puts expectations on dogs that disregard their reality.

Dogs wander in their own universe and resist being judged by human standards.

We do justice to a relationship with a dog when we honor it as it is — a dog, a creature that, for all we may understand about it, is still fraught with mystery.

Dogs are subjects in the kingdom of now,
fully present to the pulse of each moment.

Their behavioral rhythms shift as quickly as weather on
a windy day. Intense episodes of play and dominance
that express a flurry of activity in one moment organically
flow into a surrender to rest in the next. The dog knows
only the present and offers itself to it without reserve.

From a spiritual perspective there is no limit
to the change, growth and maturity that a
human being can undergo; the wonder is that,
in its own way, the same is true of the dog.

Dogs can always grow in learning
and responsiveness, in attentiveness
and bonding,

significantly broadening the parameters of what
most of us think is possible from a relationship.

In our cynical age, we somehow believe that we can go it alone, that we can be completely self-reliant; we have trouble trusting leadership.

But the dog is wiser. It knows its need for guidance and flourishes in its wake.

There is no need to apologize to a dog for taking the leadership role: all along it has been waiting for us to inspire, to be the guide along the path of companionship.

When we are quiet enough, freed
from all our inner noise and chatter,

we can see with new respect
the natural beauty and wisdom
of the world around us and
appreciate our ties to it.

Such perceptive silence opens up
our lives to a healthy reverence
and awe for all things; it creates a
capacity for openness that is
both humanizing and life-giving.

Novelty isn't always desirable in relating with a dog.
Dogs are sensitive to the security and comfort engendered
by daily rituals we hardly give a second thought to:
the morning walk, meal times, play sessions, even the quiet
togetherness of evening TV.... Such familiar patterns
stabilize the dog in a world it understands.

They also soothe the chaos of our own lives
with the peace that is their fruit.

Dogs are natural healers, often working a recuperative magic
that eludes the scope of modern medicine.

In the aftermath of trauma and unimagined loss,
the stability a dog provides through its love and
companionship can give us our life back.

How ironic that what we initially thought to be the end
of life as we knew it can become the promising beginning
of something radically new.

Dogs are not solitaries.
Their very success as a species
comes from their capacity
to form relationships,

whether in packs of their own or with human beings. From this perspective, good training is a responsibility — a true gift we can offer our dog. It is an opportunity to refine and deepen what is most natural both in the dog and in ourselves.

What is it with the fetish for dressing up dogs?

When people decorate them in outfits of human silliness, do they ever consider the canine ability to see through such mockery, or do they have any awareness at all of their dogs' feelings of discomfort and humiliation?

Dogs do not require
such vain attempts at makeover.

Their very nature possesses its own dignity, transcending any need of supplement or change. All that is required is our respect and admiration.

Fathoming the way a dog develops means recognizing
that our knowledge reflects general patterns and
not absolute rules.

We can never fully understand
why a dog is the way it is.

In fact, "the dog" does not exist — only individual dogs
and the unique way each develops.

Being authentically human means learning to give ourselves unselfishly, ungrudgingly.

Isn't it surprising how the nature of the dog evokes this from us in unique and compelling ways?

In the ordinary routine of a relationship with a dog, through the discipline and responsibility it entails, we learn about ourselves, about nature, about God and the spiritual path we are on, in ways that would otherwise be unavailable to us.

Our world is increasingly afraid of silence,
fearing the truths it whispers in our conscience.

But how silence can heal if we let it!

All good relationships — those with our dogs included —
will make room for silence, for shared moments that
transcend the need for speech. Silence allows us to take
account of ourselves, to change what is amiss, to renew
our intention to treat the other with the respect and
affection characteristic of friendship.

The root meaning
of the word obedience is "to listen."

When applied to training our dogs, it involves as much
our listening to the dog in order to discern what is
needed, as it does the dog's responding to our commands.
It involves laying aside our burdens for the moment and
entering fully into the relationship here and now so that
our word to the dog will be simple, clear, and free of
emotional or physical static.

Praise is more than treats, more than an occasional physical pat, and more than a reward for good actions.

Praise is an attitude, a stance.
Dogs who live in an atmosphere of praise come to love the human voice.

They are more trusting and accepting. They are approachable by strangers but not demanding. Dogs confident of praise from their owners do not live on the edge of an emotional abyss, always seeking attention and sulking when they do not get it. If praise is part of your attitude toward your dog, you will always have a rich and exciting relationship.

In a world choked with the disease of taking itself too seriously, dogs remind us of a more fundamental wisdom that often eludes us in our self-preoccupation. More than anything else, dogs are creatures of play, whose spontaneous interaction with life bespeaks its goodness.

Dogs become what they are through play, through
hours upon hours of undistracted merriment.
No matter how serious their adult behavior becomes
in hunting, guarding, roaming or working, the
foundation always is play. In play, they return as
to their proper home.

When we take the time and energy necessary to raise our
puppies correctly, when we learn to truly listen to them,
seeing them as they really are and guiding their
development accordingly,

a deeper part of ourselves is unlocked,
a part more compassionate and less arrogant,
more willing to share life with another life.

And whenever that happens,
we know the true meaning of happiness.

Often we blame our dogs for being disobedient when the real problem lies with us.

Being a good trainer and a good companion requires humility, the humility to realize that our own handling abilities with our dogs are continually developing, and that it is always preferable to assume first that the problem lies with us.

Inseeing is standing at the center of your dog's psyche, where your dog is a unique, individual creature, and understanding your companion from that perspective.

Inseeing is not a romantic projection of human thoughts and feelings; it takes into account the whole dog by reading what the major centers of communication are saying: ears, eyes, mouth, tail and body carriage.

Dogs and sticks: a marriage made in heaven.
Is there another object so close at hand as to
become an effortless source of delight for your dog?

A simple toss of a stick turns an ordinary walk into a game
whose strategy is to keep both of you fully engaged — your
dog placing the stick in the path of your leisurely walk, for
example, to solicit another toss; or daring you to pick it up
before lightning-fast jaws sweep it away from your grasp.

People sometimes cringe at the thought of training,
as if its purpose were to quench a dog's spirit. Nonsense.
Ultimately training is about freedom:

freedom for both ourselves
and our dogs to enjoy each other,

enhancing our relationships by allowing their potential
to blossom in the patient context of trial and error,
praise and appreciation.

Dogs love vacations as much as we do.

While there are times when it is impractical for our dogs to accompany us, we can always benefit from and revel in their spirit of playfulness and love of adventure. Just as we feel the blessed release of stress at the beach or in the woods, so, too, do our dogs. They can teach us to enjoy every moment of vacation.

The richness of the moment is everything to the dog.

The beauty, grace and elegance of the dog
point beyond themselves, bearing witness
to the deeper mystery from which they arise.

Watch a dog racing with its buddy!

You will see no consciousness in the act: the dog simply is.
But its whole being sounds a clarion call to all of us
with ears to hear.

Listen carefully to your life and you'll find that companionship with a dog touches the broader issue of our relationship with all of creation and with the Creator.

How we interact with a dog reflects our general attitude to God and nature, a tell-tale sign of the soul.

What other creature is so able to pierce
the veneer of our defenses,

reducing the gruffest human being to unselfconscious
displays of laughter and fun? By their sheer spontaneity,
dogs find our soft spots, keeping us in touch with a more
honest vision of ourselves that doesn't buy its own facade.

Dogs can be medicine for the soul.

They effortlessly take us out of ourselves, helping to keep us from becoming trapped in dark and unproductive introspection that only gives birth to alienation.

One need only look at the transforming effect dogs have in therapy work to gauge the magic they can create for all of us.

We do not find God solely in the interior realm,
and when we live our lives as if we did, we fall victim
to a dualism that has profound spiritual consequences.

Because we are responsible for them as living
creatures, needy and vulnerable, our dogs help
ground us in reality,

forcing us to appreciate the mystery of God
in all its length and breadth.

Those fortunate enough to be able
to include their dog in their work
know the impact this has on the relationship.

Subtly, without even rising to consciousness, a familiarity and
ease develop, making it difficult to imagine life without the
presence of the other — not so much a shadow as a
harmonious part of the landscape.

Over the years we've always been struck by the number of people who, all things considered, would rather spend their time with a dog than with other human beings. Though pitting dogs against humans seems unwise, it is fair to ask:

is there any other relationship in life in which the high point of the other's day is the moment we come home and walk through the door?

Consider how a dog's eyes speak.

They reflect a broad range of inner emotions that affect the
quality of our relationship, if we care enough to listen.
Joy, fear, curiosity, boredom and mischief are all reflected through
the subtlest shifts in a dog's eyes. The New Testament teaches
that "the eye is the lamp of the soul" in human beings;
the same, it can be said, holds true for dogs.

Dogs are creatures of the heart.

Their emotions are plainly before us, as if their bodies
were transparent. Dogs are unable to deceive, even if
they wanted to. Too infrequently can it be said of our
human relationships, but with a dog, what you see is
what you get. Such honesty is precious, creating a trust
that never turns on us.

Is it any wonder that we treasure our
connection with them?

The biggest problem with dogs is that they don't live long enough. They always seem to leave us when we're most vulnerable, most in need of their biased, affirming presence.

Dogs make us believe
we can actually be as they see us,

and it's often only when they're gone that we realize their role in what we've become.

Do the bonds of relationship extend beyond this life?
We have no proof, one way or another. But there is
a depth to our experience that awakens faith, faith
that in the mysterious character of life ultimately
nothing of real value will ever be lost.

Our closest relationships, both with humans
and with dogs, somehow point beyond
themselves, leading us to hope that there is
indeed something of the eternal present in them.

acknowledgments

This book expresses a deep intuition that is very dear to our community. We delight in the mystery that binds dogs with human beings and are grateful to all who have used their gifts to make this book a reality. In a special way we'd like to thank Vincent Remini for his beautiful photography and patient attention to his craft, our editor and dear friend Kate Hartson who has overseen this entire project, Michael Hentges, whose design of the book sings with joy, and Bob Somerville who did a helpful copyedit to all the meditations.

Finally, we thank all the owners and the wonderful dogs and people who grace these pages, with special acknowledgment to the dogs of Canine Companions for Independence and the work they do, to Captain James Van Thach, USA (Ret.) for his service to our country, to Lance and Kimberly Blanchard and their dachshunds, and to the Southampton Animal Shelter for helping us shine a light on dog adoption.

Best wishes to you,
The Monks of New Skete

about the monks of new skete

The Monks of New Skete have lived as a community in Cambridge, New York, for more than four decades. They support themselves by breeding, raising and training dogs at their monastery. Their widely praised books *How to Be Your Dog's Best Friend*, *The Art of Raising a Puppy*, *Divine Canine*, *Dogs & Devotion* and *In the Spirit of Happiness* have sold well over a million copies.

www.newskete.org